Fill My Cup, Lord

Marian Kay Walton

"Sow with a view to righteousness.
Reap in accordance with kindness.
Break up your fallow ground,
it is time to seek the Lord, until
He comes to rain righteousness on you"
(Hosea 10:12, NASB).

ASPECT Books

www.ASPECTBooks.com

ISBN-13: 978-1-57258-855-4 (Paperback)
ISBN-13: 978-1-57258-856-1 (ePub)
ISBN-13: 978-1-57258-857-8 (Kindle/Mobi)

Library of Congress Control Number: 2012913596

Published by
ASPECT Books

www.ASPECTBooks.com

Acknowledgment

Thank you to my God and my Lord,
the Almighty Father on the throne;
Jesus, the Lamb; and
the Holy Spirit of understanding.

Table of Contents

1

An Invitation

We all know that we are to stay connected to the Vine. This is the desire of our hearts. Yet, I personally am appalled at the rapidity with which I fall flat on my face and fail to bear witness to God's love. Through the ministry of 3ABN faithfully sowing seeds of righteousness, my desire to learn more about the Bible grew. I determined that there was no going forward in my walk with Christ unless I found a way to retain a serious amount of scripture.

My dad is a language teacher, and he often refers to the importance of associating meaning with learning. Knowing the difficulties people have learning a foreign language, I thought that that situation sounded like the challenge I was having learning scripture. I knew I needed to identify the reasons why I fell so fast and connect the scriptures in a way that deepened the meaning of the message enough for me to be able to cogitate on the Word. In this way, I could start to connect the dots between morning and evening worship.

I would like to invite you to experience the interest that the Lord has in our memorization of Scripture. If you ask Him to fill your cup with His Word, He will answer your prayer.

2

More Memory

Have you ever wished you had a better memory, more brainpower? There are ways to do this. Your memory is a product of the health of such organs as the heart and lungs. This is good news because it means there are a number of ways to stimulate the memory and increase its level of activity.

Memory includes storing, retaining, and recalling information. Part of the memory is for short-term task-based conditions. In this book, we will be discussing long-term memory and how to recall portions of the wonderful things the Lord has given us in His Word.

> O Lord, You have searched me and known me.... You scrutinize my path and my lying down, and are intimately acquainted with all my ways.... You have enclosed me behind and before, and laid Your hand

> upon me.... Search me, O God, and know my heart; try me and know my anxious thoughts; and see if there be any hurtful way in me, and lead me in the everlasting way (Ps. 139:1-5, 23, 24, NASB).

We establish new content in our minds by association with emotions and already stored experiences and facts. Long-term memory may store large quantities of information for as long as a lifetime. Through repetition and association, scriptures may be stored for future use—this is done by making permanent changes to the brain. The more meaning attached to the subject, the more widely it is disseminated in the regions of the brain. This results in more surface area from which to retrieve the information.

Important functions of the memory are in the frontal lobe where your ability to make judgments is also located. Because of this, stimulants and toxic substances need to be eliminated from the lifestyle in order to enhance memory. Although substances, such as caffeine may increase some mental activity, it may interfere with the use of wide-range mental functioning and processing. In addition, temporary or permanent memory loss may occur from exposure to toxic substances or chemical imbalances. Cerebral-vascular disease brought on by cardiovascular or respiratory illness also affects memory loss.

The condition of the memory is a reflection of the state of the rest of the body. So we need to seek out those practices that will increase our health. How does health affect the memory? It is the process that restores the intended high level of functioning encoded in the genetic code.

By far the best liquid to use to increase brainpower is water. The hydrolytic and hydroelectric sources of energy are impaired without the benefits of readily available H_2O. Water also has an adhesive quality that helps to bond and organize cellular and tissue architecture. This remarkable thirst-quencher is the best solvent to prevent proteins from getting tangled as happens with Alzheimer's disease. Adequate hydration ensures the proper transportation of the oxygen we breathe and the nerve impulses of the body. We are well on our way to improving our memory, when we drink an adequate amount of water each day.

One more way to improve circulation in the body is to breathe deeply. Deep breathing is known as a stress reliever because of its ability to enrich the cells with more oxygen. The idea is to allow for the fullest expansion of the lungs by allowing the diaphragm to expand toward the abdomen. This increases the taking in of oxygen and a corresponding increased exhalation of CO_2. Besides consciously breathing better, exercise and stretching are also good ways to increase air exchange by helping to loosen tight muscles and nerves.

An understanding of the digestive process will also help us apply good health principles to promote a good memory. Healing enzymes and energy levels are decreased by eating in excess. We need to be careful not to give the stomach a load that requires more energy to process than it actually provides for the body. This means eating smaller portions than we are used to, and it requires us to stop before the sense of hunger is gone. Top off a meal with a refreshing, gentle walk! The human body draws on more than the products of digestion for its energy sources. Water and oxygen play important roles in the energy processes of the body. So, the next time you feel weak, try more fresh air and water.

The appetite may be educated to the point that the body relishes good food more than it ever did the stimulating fare. First, we need to deal with the cold hard fact that hunger pangs are not the body's emergency response alarm for starvation. Actually, hunger is easy to educate and control. Eating only at set times five to six hours apart will reduce the incidence of hunger pangs. If you cannot fit three meals into a day, two meals will do. When we eat plant-based foods, it will satisfy our body and improve our health. Also, providing plenty of variety promotes satisfaction. In addition, foods high in B vitamins increase energy and are a part of the support group for our exhausted neurons in the memory department.

> Grains, fruits, nuts, and vegetables constitute the diet chosen for us by our Creator. These foods prepared in as simple and natural a manner as possible, are the most healthful and nourishing. They impart a strength, a power of endurance, and a vigor of intellect, that are not afforded by a more complex and stimulating diet (Ellen G. White, *Counsels on Diet and Foods*, p. 310).

We read about Jesus surviving in the wilderness for forty days, John the Baptist living on carob pods, and the children of Israel eating manna for forty years. These are all forms of fasting, or it could be said, simplifying the diet. Could it be that the Lord did not intend that eating should hold a primary role in our lives as it does today? Yes, the social aspect is heart-warming, but I do not think this means consuming rich foods that harm our bodies. By relieving the body of relentless digestive processes, the body is able to divert the energy toward our emotional and thought-processing centers. Fasting does not have to be abstinence from food. Calorie restrictions and eating foods higher in nutritive qualities is enough to receive great benefit while still maintaining a regular meal schedule.

It is good to be aware of the brain's requirements. Twenty percent of our daily calories go to the brain, but the brain only accounts for 2 percent of the body's weight. The liver stores glucose and will keep the brain supplied if all is well. We need not try to make up for any perceived deficits by eating snacks. This triggers an immune response that may cause cognitive deficits, and too much sugar raises cortisol, which impairs memory.

The brain is composed of 60 percent fat. But people who eat animal fat are more prone to mental decline. Instead, seeds and nuts are good brain food. A good carob brownie with seeds and nuts is a good natural food to give the brain what it needs.

The body has a wide variety of functions, such as digestion, respiration, and immune response. But there is one function we rarely hear about and that is cleansing. The whole body cooperates with this duty. Through unhealthy practices there is a build-up of waste products. But the systems will catch up with a change in lifestyle. In this way restoration may be a slow, gentle process. It is important to support the body's efforts to keep a clean house. This includes not eating anything that is harmful to the body. Eating appropriate amounts and eating on a strict schedule help the body work more efficiently. These good habits will prevent a backlog of toxins that cannot be eliminated in the normal processes.

We have so much to be grateful for. With practice we will realize how closely the Lord watches us and how personalized are the blessings in our lives. Gratitude is truly the breath of life to the child of God. What were you thinking, Lord, when you made someone such as I? Something so intricate and ornamental as the human body is truly meant to be no less than a temple of the living God.

References:

- "Memory Loss," "Frontal Lobe," "Memory," Wikipedia, http://wikipedia.org (accessed May 8, 2012).
- "Renew – Stress on the Brain," The Franklin Institute Online, http://www.fi.edu/learn/brain/stress.html#stressmemory (accessed June 11, 2012).

- Fereydoon Batmanghelidj, M.D., *Your Body's Many Cries for Water* (Vienna, VA: Global Health Solutions, Inc., 1995).

- Robin Nixon, "Brain Food: How to Eat Smart," Live Science, http://www.livescience.com/3186-brain-food-eat-smart.html (accessed May 8, 2012).

3

Memory and Meaning

One of the educational advances of the twentieth century was the change from learning by rote, or stark memorization, to an understanding of the role of establishing meaning in the learning process. It is with this awareness that we may begin to learn how to memorize scripture. The primary reason for adopting scripture into our lives is so that we may move from the everyday things to breathing the heavenly atmosphere. I have always admired my dad's steadfastness and courage, and I believe his character is a testimony of the Word stored in his heart.

We have plenty to keep us busy, but we often operate on autopilot. And when we do, we somehow end up tripping over ourselves or putting our foot in our mouth. Is it that we are living without God's goodness that provides shade in the heat of the hour and warmth in the chill of the moment? It is the Lord's desire that we would always recognize His help and provision for every need. Let's keep the light on for Him. When we prepare our hearts to beat as one with God's Word, we recognize God's involvement in our life and seek to develop our character to match His. As we grow closer to God, the natural response to His love will be a quest to conquer the strongholds of sin and bring others near to the heart of God.

When you sit down to learn scripture, I recommend that you look for what applies to your life instead of just pulling a verse out of a hat. Select verses that will heal and strengthen the weaknesses in your life—plug the biggest holes in the dike first.

In that way, you first establish the meaning for why you want to learn the verse enough to remember it in its entirety. As you start to do this, you may look at the words with the mind's eye. This, we have discovered, deepens the understanding.

Of course, the very process of learning scripture stimulates the brain and increases your capacity to learn more. Thanks to medical research, we now know that new brain cells continue to form throughout a person's lifetime. This means we may adapt and change even into old age. So we have nothing to fear when we hear the word memorization. It is just a form of exercise for the brain. But approaching the task in an interesting way will engage you and help you to look forward to the next time.

Chunking is a device used for memorization. This involves breaking up the passage into interesting chunks and seeing how they relate to each other. It takes about eight seconds of undisturbed focus to move a piece of information from short-term to long-term memory. Spend time relating the cluster of words to information and experiences you already have stored away. Share and explain the concepts to someone else in your own words. When you have a verse memorized, recite it several more times in the same day so as to engrain it in your long-term memory. Reviewing the passage at spaced intervals is better than trying to have it fully memorized in one sitting.

When you first start to exercise your memory, ask the Holy Spirit to bring to mind stories or verses that you need to apply to your life. We tend to think of memorization as something that is just up to us. But, remember, the Holy Spirit is ready and waiting to engage with us and focus our hearts and minds on heavenly things. The Holy Spirit brings within our reach and impresses our minds with the concepts that each of us individually needs to move forward in service to our Lord and those around us.

As I have embarked on my own journey to memorize scripture, I have chosen verses ahead of time for different occasions. I have found it particularly helpful to have verses memorized that will restore my soul when I find myself in the doldrums. These same verses work on the prevention side when I recognize a looming problem. The following three texts I have found helpful when I need to recall the Lord's provision and portion in my life.

> The Lord is my portion (Ps. 119:57, NASB).

> Not to us, O Lord, not to us, but to Your name give glory, because of Your lovingkindness, because of Your truth (Ps. 115:1, NASB).

> The Lord's lovingkindnesses indeed never cease, for His compassions never fail. They are new every morning. Great is Your faithfulness (Lam. 3:22, 23, NASB).

Reference:

- Earl W. Stevick, *Memory, Meaning, and Method: Some Psychological Perspectives on Language Learning* (Boston, MA: Heinle ELT, 1996).

4

Let's Learn

Starting a new project such as learning scriptures is like forming a new habit. Most new habits are formed by repetition. But a habit that will affect our character development will require more. The biological definition of a habit is "the tendency to grow in a certain way." A plant's growth depends on the soil moisture and the sun. We have all seen a plant growing toward the sunlight. This is what learning Bible verses does for humans. It helps us turn to the Son.

So, let's think about what kind of environment we need to nurture this new habit. Prayer sets the stage for any changes we want to make. It opens the door to His presence and keeps us connected to the Holy Spirit. Asking forgiveness for our sins and in turn forgiving others keeps the rocks out of the soil of our life. Shifting away from worldly distractions and looking at things through the Lord's eyes is nourishing. Sharing our holy outlook with others keeps the ground soft.

Remember, our human tendency is to do what is familiar. But if what is familiar is not good for us, we need to make changes. Change takes time and will not happen overnight. Simple habits like drinking more water take three weeks to become automatic. But complex changes may take two or more months to become familiar. A recent study done at the University of London showed that it is the early efforts that have the best results for stimulating change. Putting forth the effort when it is least comfortable sets a solid foundation for forming a new habit.

Making the initial effort can be a challenge. But the Lord promises that those who hunger and thirst for righteousness will be satisfied. Learning scripture is a project that will encompass your whole day. That is why I wrote this book. I wanted to make scripture readily available and divided into specific topics to assist in memorizing and drinking deeply from the water of life anytime and anywhere.

The way we learn depends on our senses of sight and hearing. This is how we process most information. Understanding the differences in the way we learn can help in our communication as well as in our learning. With practice, people can then learn from you. Also, with an awareness of your learning habits, you may identify other ways of learning and incorporate new and fresh approaches to expand your resources for learning.

Visual learning involves taking notes, writing in a journal, or closing your eyes to visualize the words and create pictures in your mind from what you've read. Diagrams and concept maps allow visual learners to link words and ideas to help them understand difficult concepts. This also helps to establish patterns and connect new ideas to familiar ideas. Memorizing a piece of information by closing your eyes and trying to visualize it is a type of visual learning. Reading straight through the material to get the context and the "big picture" is a good way to start. Then continue by highlighting especially meaningful passages. Amplifying this information by taking notes or writing in a journal further prepares the mind for recalling the passage word for word.

Auditory learning involves listening and speaking. Reading instructions out loud helps to develop the understanding. The expression and emphasis that is added when reading a passage is also helpful to grasp the full meaning. Having soft instrumental music in the background is one more way to increase variety during study time and is helpful for some people to be able to focus and concentrate on the words. Recording scripture and listening to it while doing another activity is also helpful.

Regardless of your learning style, having a partner, whether it be a family member, church member, or friend, to encourage you has great benefits and rewards. The Lord also offers us encouragement in His Word as to the joys and rewards of learning His Word.

> If you abide in Me, and My words abide in you, ask whatever you wish, and it will be done for you (John 15:7, NASB).

> Do not store up for yourselves treasures on earth, where moth and rust destroy ... But store up for yourselves treasures in heaven ... for where your treasure is, there your heart will be also (Matt. 6:19-21, NASB).

> Therefore everyone who hears these words of Mine and acts on them, may be compared to a wise man who built his house on the rock (Matt. 7:24, NASB).

Adapting new learning strategies takes some getting used to and happens in stages. For example, many babies do not like to take a bath. But if you gradually get them used to water, soon they are taking bubble baths and playing in the tub. When we store information in our brain, we have the ability to recall it for later use. We may do this in several ways. We may recall the stored information when looking for the meaning of something, trying to explain something, evaluating our choices, or examining the big picture of a situation. By using a wide range of methods to learn, you will make the most of your learning potential. And with practice it becomes easier to assimilate new information.

The brain uses dopamine to reward us for making good choices so that we will repeat the process. When we are learning something new or starting a good habit, it is important to identify the benefits and think about them. This helps to establish the automatic dopamine response that will help to keep us coming back to the next close encounter with the Word. Once we have stored information about the scriptures we want to learn and started to cogitate about it, we are ready to start learning it word for word.

References:

- Phillippa Lally, et al., "How are habits formed: Modeling habit formation in the real world," *European Journal of Social Psychology* 40 (2010): pp. 998-1009.

- "Visual Learning," "Auditory Learning," Wikipedia, http://wikipedia.org (accessed May 8, 2012).

5

My Sanctuary

I go to my sanctuary every morning. This is where I pray and read my Bible and seek His presence. It may start with a quiet moment before I begin studying the Scripture. Sometimes in the stillness I remember something I did or said the day before. It is then that I ask for forgiveness and for Jesus to cover me with His blood concerning these wrongs.

Do you know what I mean when I say sanctuary? Webster's defines it as a place of refuge or protection, immunity from punishment. This is what my morning devotional time with the Lord is for me. It bears likeness to the tabernacle in the wilderness, which was replaced by the temple in Jerusalem. These were both patterned after the sanctuary in heaven. The earthly sanctuaries were to represent God's desire to be with us. The final result of God dwelling with us is our allegiance to everything holy and our separation from the false.

> [Jesus] has taken His seat at the right hand of the throne of the Majesty in the heavens, a minister in the sanctuary (Heb. 8:1, 2, NASB).

> At night my soul longs for You, indeed, my spirit within me seeks You diligently; for when the earth experiences Your judgments the inhabitants of the world learn righteousness (Isa. 26:9, NASB).

> To love Him with all the heart and with all the understanding and with all the strength, and to love one's neighbor as himself, is much more than all burnt offerings and sacrifices (Mark 12:33, NASB).

> May He send you help from the sanctuary (Ps. 20:2, NASB).

My sanctuary time in His presence includes enjoying restful peace with my heavenly Father. This is also when He communicates with me. It is a time of letting go of burdens and feelings and giving Him complete control. A time of worship in the morning prepares me to start the day. Then every hour I touch base with Him through scripture and prayer. In between these times I think on the significance of the "spiritual snack" and thank Him for the blessings in the present. This defragments my thought processes throughout the day so that I may stay true to my early morning plan to let go and let God.

A big spiritual breakfast prepares me to let go of my cultivated and inherited patterns of behavior. This is time to reprogram my response mechanisms by putting new information into my system. It is also a time to receive wisdom and ideas and assurance for the day ahead. Indeed this is a blessed hour.

Do we realize how respectful He is of us and our choices? Let's do an about face and humble ourselves and come to God. He is calling us. Minimize the affairs of this world. Maximize the concerns of the eternal kingdom. Often it is a matter of now versus eternity. The intensity of this contest is matched by no other. The outcome of this drama is in our hands. Decide which one to starve and which one to feed: carnal desires that fragment every noble aspiration or holy ambitions that will replace that which is eating away at the fabric of our lives.

Do not be led astray by lies. In order to do this we need to wrestle with the idea of truth. What is it? Where is it? Why does it matter? Have you ever lost a key that you needed to open a door? When you were trying to remember where it was last, did you tell yourself, it is okay, it doesn't matter? Or did you agonize about the truth of what happened? When you found the key, I'm sure you rejoiced because you did not have to make another key or pay for a locksmith or miss work or an appointment. Wouldn't you like to have keys for other parts of your life? This is what the Bible has within its pages. Once and for all, you can have contentment and peace that cannot be shaken, and you will have enough to share with your loved ones and strangers too. Let's learn to love God because then we will be able to understand how to love our neighbor.

How do we show respect for Someone who created us and this world? For Jesus who laid down His life to save us from our sins? When we think of all the vast starry sky, we say, "What is man, that You ... are concerned about him?" (Heb. 2:6, NASB). He is all about relationships, not size or sparkle. That is why everything in our life is of paramount importance to the Lord. This is why He was willing to leave His comfort zone and come down to this earth to be a part of humanity so that we could know Him as He really is and not have to take someone else's word for it. This is still true today.

My experience has always been that all things do work together for good to those that follow Him (Rom. 8:28). The summer after college, I worked as a maid at Many Glacier Hotel in Glacier National Park, Montana. What a beautiful place! It was like a paid vacation. Well, one of my friends there was the baker. At the end of the summer, we decided to follow a goat trail to a glacial lake. It was recommended as a good hike. The funny thing was that on our way back we could not find the goat trail, and there were no cell phones then. With her being an avowed atheist, I did not pray at first. But after spending the night on the mountain and waking up to snow falling, I didn't care if it bothered her; I prayed out loud with every ounce of strength. This is how the rescuers found us. They heard me from the trail beneath us and sent a helicopter. From that experience, my friend said she learned something about God. Was it worth it? The Lord knows the end from the beginning. His ways are mysterious, and if we do not understand in the here and now, we will in eternity.

Yes, it is the most natural thing in life to respect our God who cares about us so much. We love Him because He first loved us. The more we learn about Him, the more we are enveloped in peace and joy and we set our face like flint to follow Him closely. We learn that the antics of this world are meant to divert us from partaking of God the Father who wants to bind us to Himself forever. Whether we know it or not, God is on trial in the hearts of those around us. Let us show them that we trust God so they may learn about His love and store His promises in their memory too.

6

Written on the Heart

Recent research indicates that the heart has a memory. Is it not the heart that binds us to each other? It is not the heart that gets broken and needs to be healed after certain hurtful relationships? What is a person to do to heal the heart or win back another's affections? We ask the question, "How may we bind the heart, during the storms of life, to the ship's mast, Jesus Christ?"

If it isn't relationships gone bad, the world tries to steal the affections of the heart and fragment the deepest longings. On every level, from perfume to expensive clothes, the world around us clamors for our interest as it jumps from conquest to conquest.

A longing for peace and security hopefully drives us to open the Bible. No other book meets the multi-faceted requirements of the heart. Here is where we find recorded the cry of our Savior at Gethsemane, "Not my will, but thine, be done" (Luke 22:42). It was His love for us and His desire for us to be united with the Father that enabled Him to endure the cross. This is the love that we as disciples are seeking. The divine purpose of memorizing the Word of God is to help us cultivate the fruits of the Spirit and to bear these fruits in our lives—love, patience, temperance, kindness, etc.—under any circumstances.

Let us look more at this heart of God that we are seeking for ourselves. Picture Eden, dripping with every nuance of tenderness and appeal to maintain a close relationship with the Creator. But then sin entered the picture. What grand compassion is displayed with His gentle utterance to the man, "Where are you?" (Gen. 3:9, NASB). Even as Adam portrayed the cruel face of sin, by responding, "The woman whom You gave to be with me, she gave me from the tree, and I ate" (Gen. 3:12, NASB). The Lord responded graciously to his statement before turning to Eve to address her. God knew full well that Adam was equally responsible for sin. Instead of laying out in lurid detail the folly of what Adam had done, He prepared Adam and Eve for the eminent consequences looming on the horizon. Before the painful reality set in, He wanted them to know that God had made provision even for the choice of the disdain for His goodness that they demonstrated.

The serpent deliberately asked Eve a question to get her to engage in conversation. Eve answered. We have the advantage of knowing that this was a mistake. When we find ourselves in such a position, we need to turn away and flee to a place where we can hear the Lord's voice.

Moses wanted to see God's glory. This, the Lord said, was His goodness. But because His goodness is so dynamic, Moses could not look Him in the face and live. What is it about God that is so fiery and consuming? He is the source of all creation, the One who knits the flesh to the bones, puts a twinkle in the eye, and causes the bee to buzz. This all flows out from Him in a constant flood of life. Is it any wonder that the Lord covered Moses with His hand until He had passed by, only allowing Moses to see His back. Yet, this was enough that Moses' face shone from beholding the Lord.

The people of Israel likewise were not able to look at Moses' face. He had to cover it with a veil. Moses had gone through the process of parting from the ways of the world for forty years in preparation to be used by the Lord to lead the children of Israel through the same process. There must have been a time that Moses reflected back on his own wilderness experience and the patience of God in dealing with him. This is why he knew that it was in God's heart to do the same for a whole nation.

The Lord covets our best interests and is willing to shield us even from Himself and His great goodness to protect us from death. Let us say with the hymn writer, "More, more about Jesus."

Do you remember that Elijah wanted to die? Yet, God took him to heaven in a flash of splendor, and Elijah never saw death. The earth could not contain all the books that could be written on the interventions and provisions of God for His wandering children. Are we willing to have Him write His law of love on our heart?

> For this is the covenant that I will make with the house of Israel after those days, says the Lord: I will put My laws into their minds, and I will write them on their hearts. And I will be their God, and they shall be My people (Heb. 8:10, NASB).

> You are a letter of Christ, cared for by us, written not with ink but with the Spirit of the living God, not on tablets of stone but on tablets of

> human hearts (2 Cor. 3:3, NASB).

As we approach the borders of the Promised Land, will we turn back in fear and distrust of God? Or will we surrender all for the sake of the knowledge of His will? It is His will that will lead us through, not our own. Let us drink often from the Word and "stand up, stand up for Jesus" and His ways.

Reference:

- Paul Pearsall, Ph.D., *The Heart's Code: Tapping the Wisdom and Power of Our Heart Energy* (New York, NY: Broadway Books, 1999).

7

The Struggle

Learning to memorize scripture and stay connected to God's Word is a big change that involves biochemical rearrangement of the human fabric of our being. That takes time, because it is a makeover of our lifestyle. Even the best changes cause stress. So expect upheaval in three areas: ourselves, our family, and our friends. While we are taking the logs out of our own eyes by learning scripture, we need to pray for love beyond compare for those around us. It also means we should avoid engaging in controversies. We will learn to remain quiet when conflict arises until the Holy Spirit gives us the right words and actions.

Sometimes I am in anguish about something, and I barely know what to think. Then I remember that I must wait in my self-made bottomless pit for the Lord to give me the answer. All my righteousness is filthy rags, and I dare not make a move until I am assured of

His guiding presence. While I am waiting, I remember how He has led in the past and that He always knows what is best. He is ready and waiting with His unfathomable love, waiting for me to present this anguish to Him. Then I realize, deep in my heart, I am thinking, *He is going to punish me and make me suffer unbearably over this matter.* When I confess this thought and ask for forgiveness, a sweet answer lifts me out of the cold darkness.

We are not memorizing scripture or daily drinking from His cup for only our own peace and contentment but for the benefit of those around us. As we deepen our relationship with God, we may find ourselves thrust into seemingly impossible situations for others. Go where humility and service take you. We need to be willing to be drawn into the lives of others, to feel their pain so we may know where to apply the balm of truth, when and where the Holy Spirit directs. As we memorize scriptures, we will be able to offer words of encouragement to those around us.

You may feel too weak to minister to others, but the Lord literally lifts us up and gives us the strength to go forward. Thirty years ago I had boils that would not go away, and I hardly slept for a year. Even the emergency room staff I saw said there was nothing they could do for someone in my condition. I had heard that

Jesus is the Great Physician. I asked Him if He would be my doctor, and He led me through the trial. I knew that the one thing I could not afford to do was give up. I had to keep moving in His strength. This meant being willing to wait for my needs to be met while ministering to others that were suffering. Don't ask me how He does it, but I know from experience that it works.

On the other hand, your family and friends may not understand your desire to draw close to the Lord through His Word. You may have to withstand ridicule and teasing as you dedicate time to memorize God's Word. Stand firm. If the pressure mounts and you feel yourself slipping, simply say, "Hold me, Lord." He knows what you mean. In the midst of trials, the Word of God is your lifeline.

As you read through the remainder of the book, my prayer is that you will find the topics I have selected and the corresponding scriptures to be a blessing and an encouragement as you hide God's Word in your heart.

As I recommended in another chapter, I believe that you will find great success in memorizing scriptures that address what you are going through. If you are struggling with loving others, focus on texts that talk about love. If you are having a hard time with the Sabbath, search out scriptures that talk about the Sabbath and commit them to memory. If you are finding it difficult to be joyful in all circumstances, look up texts that talk about the joy of the Lord and His will for our lives. Above all, Lord, teach us to believe in your Word and hide it in our hearts.

8

We Believe

To believe or not to believe, that is the question. “How blessed is the man who does not walk in the counsel of the wicked” (Ps. 1:1, NASB). We live in an age of relativism, where our religion is based on what makes us comfortable and does not cause problems. This results in a mix of good and evil because God will not impose Himself on us. However the assailant of all that is good creates an endless spectrum of problems from daily annoyances to life-threatening situations to break our trust in God.

Unfortunately, the resulting separation from God will drain all life from our existence. It is like when a car runs out of oil, you may keep running the engine, but soon the parts are no longer able to function because of the prolonged friction. God is holy. There is no shadow of error with Him. He desires only what is good for us. He wants to cover us, surround us, and shield us from all evil, and this He can and will do when we spend time in His Word, learning the counsel of the godly. When God moves into our lives and becomes a part of our everyday existence, we become aware of what needs to be changed and where we need to apply the healing balm of His Word. Now instead of being in the camp of those who don’t care about life, we are in the sanctuary of God’s protection, and we are part of the solution instead of being part of the problem.

We are part of the controversy of good versus evil whether we like it or not. You have the ability to decide who is going to win the greatest contest of all time, the battle for a human soul—you! On one side there is the claim that you will do just fine without Jesus, and on the other, there is the comfort, guidance, and healing that comes from association with the Creator. As the final days of earth's history come to a close, we must make a choice as to who we will serve. If you choose to follow God, do it with your whole heart and commit to establishing a firm relationship with Him so that you may withstand the trials of life.

I AM

When Moses asked the Lord, "Who should I say sent me?", the Lord said, "Say that I AM sent you" (see Exod. 3:14). As we read through the Bible, we discover more about the great I AM.

> "I am the Alpha and the Omega," says the Lord God, "who is, and who was, and who is to come, the Almighty" (Rev. 1:8, NIV).

> Is there any God besides Me, or is there any other Rock? I know of

> none (Isa. 44:8, NASB).
>
> Come unto me, all ye that labour and are heavy laden, and I will give you rest. Take my yoke upon you, and learn of me; for I am meek and lowly in heart: and ye shall find rest unto your souls. For my yoke is easy, and my burden is light (Matt. 11:28).
>
> And let the one who is thirsty come; let the one who wishes take the water of life without cost (Rev. 22:17, NASB).
>
> Let him come to Me and drink (John 7:37, NASB).
>
> Blessed are they which do hunger and thirst after righteousness: for they shall be filled (Matt. 5:6).

Sabbath Delight

One Sabbath as I sat on the front steps, I watched the rays of the setting sun deepen the greens of our patch of lawn, and I thought, "This is delight."

> God blessed the seventh day, and sanctified it (Gen. 2:3).

> He makes me lie down in green pastures; He leads me beside quiet waters. He restores my soul; He guides me in the paths of righteousness for His name's sake (Ps. 23:2, 3, NASB).

> For as the earth brings forth its sprouts, and as a garden causes the things sown in it to spring up, so the Lord God will cause righteousness and praise to spring up before all the nations (Isa. 61:11, NASB).

Jesus, the Son of God

As the Son of God and the Son of man, Jesus is the bond who draws us to look upward.

> In the beginning was the Word, and the Word was with God, and the Word was God (John 1:1).

> ... being the brightness of his glory, and the express image of his person, and upholding all things by the word of his power (Heb. 1:3).

> "You shall call His name Jesus, for He will save His people from their sins.... And they shall call His

> name Immanuel," which translated means, "God with us" (Matt. 1:21, 23 NASB).

> And the Word was made flesh, and dwelt among us ... full of grace and truth (John 1:14, KJ21).

> Christ *was* faithful as a Son over His house (Heb. 3:6, NASB).

By His Spirit

We need the touch of the Holy Spirit on our hearts and those around us. Let us seek that which invites God's company.

> I will pour out ... the Spirit of grace and of supplication, so that they will look on Me whom they have pierced; and they will mourn for Him (Zech. 12:10, NASB).

> Be careful how you walk (Eph. 5:15, NASB).

> Walk ... with all lowliness and meekness, with longsuffering, forbearing one another in love (Eph. 4:1, 2).

> The wind blows where it wishes and you hear the sound of it, but

> do not know where it comes from and where it is going; so is everyone who is born of the Spirit (John 3:8, NASB).

Holy, Holy, Holy

When we look to God, we see that He is so appealing and dear. Envision the rainbow around His throne, the bow of promise that He wants to share with us for our comfort and pleasure. I want Him to be my God!

> There before me was a throne in heaven with someone sitting on it. And the one who sat there had the appearance of jasper and carnelian. A rainbow, resembling an emerald, encircled the throne (Rev. 4:2, 3, NIV).

> As the appearance of the rainbow in the clouds on a rainy day, so was the appearance of the surrounding radiance. Such was the appearance of the likeness of the glory of the Lord (Ezek. 1:28, NASB).

> And God said, ... I do set my bow in the cloud, and it shall be for a token of a covenant between me and

the earth (Gen. 9:13).

Savior

By watching our Savior, we see that He walked through the doldrums of life on this earth and carved a new path for us that gives us a new direction.

> To Jerusalem, 'I will give a messenger of good news.' ... Behold, My Servant, whom I uphold; My chosen one in whom My soul delights. I have put My Spirit upon Him;... He will not be disheartened or crushed" (Isa. 41:27-42:4, NASB).

> Behold, the Lamb of God who takes away the sin of the world (John 1:29, NASB).

> Large crowds followed Him from Galilee ... and Jerusalem ... and from beyond the Jordan.... He opened His mouth and began to teach them, saying, "Blessed are the poor in spirit, for theirs is the kingdom of heaven" (Matt. 4:25-5:3, NASB).

> Be of good cheer; it is I; be not afraid (Matt. 14:27).

> We have seen today that God speaks with man, yet he lives (Deut. 5:24, NASB).

The Mysteries of the Kingdom

The will of God is to share His goodness with us and those around us, now and forever.

> Whoever does the will of My Father who is in heaven, he is My brother and sister and mother (Matt. 12:50, NASB).

> I will give you the keys of the kingdom of heaven (Matt. 16:19, NASB).

> The good man brings good things out of the good stored up in him (Matt. 12:35, NIV).

> Then shall the righteous shine forth as the sun in the kingdom of their Father (Matt. 13:43).

The Father

The Lord is the ultimate Father, and we are His children. We have a lot to look forward to.

On that which resembled a throne, high up, was a figure with the appearance of a man. (Ezek. 1:26, NASB).

He who sits on the throne said, “Behold, I am making all things new” (Rev. 21:5, NASB).

In keeping with his promise we are looking forward to a new heaven and a new earth, the home of righteousness (2 Peter 3:13, NIV).

For the Lord himself shall descend from heaven with a shout... (1 Thess. 4:16).

And it shall be said in that day, Lo, this is our God; we have waited for him, and he will save us: this is the LORD; we have waited for him, we will be glad and rejoice in his salvation (Isa. 25:9).

There Is a Bridge to Heaven

I have heard of bridges that claim to be connected to heaven that really go nowhere. But there is a true Bridge to heaven.

Behold, a ladder was set on the

> earth with its top reaching to heaven; and behold, the angels of God were ascending and descending on it. And behold, the Lord stood above it and said, "I am the Lord, the God of your father Abraham (Gen. 28:12, 13, NASB).

> [Stephen], being full of the Holy Ghost, looked up stedfastly into heaven, and saw the glory of God, and Jesus standing on the right hand of God (Acts 7:55).

> And to Him was given dominion, glory and a kingdom, that all the peoples, nations and men of every language might serve Him.... But the saints of the Highest One will receive the kingdom and possess the kingdom forever, for all ages to come (Dan. 7:14, 18, NASB).

Our Part

The Lord has opened the windows of heaven for our blessing—the kind of blessing that prompts us to lend a helping hand.

> "Is it not to divide your bread with the hungry and bring the homeless

> poor into the house; when you see the naked, to cover him; and not to hide yourself from your own flesh? Then your light will break out like the dawn, and your recovery will speedily spring forth; ... Then you will call, and the Lord will answer; You will cry, and He will say, 'Here I am.' If you remove the yoke from your midst, the pointing of the finger and speaking wickedness, and if you give yourself to the hungry and satisfy the desire of the afflicted, then your light will rise in darkness and your gloom will become like midday.... And you will be like a watered garden (Isa. 58:7-11, NASB).

> Truly I say to you, to the extent that you did it to one of these brothers of Mine, even the least of them, you did it to Me (Matt. 25:40, NASB).

The Lord's Baptism

Faithful in the beginning, middle, and the end of His life, we can trust Him to be our example.

> Then Jesus arrived from Galilee at

> the Jordan coming to John, to be baptized by him. But John tried to prevent Him, saying, "I have need to be baptized by You, and do You come to me?" But Jesus answering said to him, "Permit it at this time; for in this way it is fitting for us to fulfill all righteousness" (Matt. 3:13-15, NASB).

> Corresponding to that, baptism now saves you—not the removal of dirt from the flesh, but an appeal to God for a good conscience—through the resurrection of Jesus Christ (1 Peter 3:21, NASB).

> Now when all the people were baptized, Jesus was also baptized (Luke 3:21, NASB).

The Word

The Word of Christ is more than words on a page, it is the fabric of life itself.

> The Lord is my shepherd; I shall not want (Ps. 23:1).

> I have esteemed the words of his mouth more than my necessary food (Job 23:12).

Not in words taught by human wisdom, but in those taught by the Spirit, combining spiritual thoughts with spiritual words (1 Cor. 2:13, NASB).

By them Your servant is warned; in keeping them there is great reward (Ps. 19:11, NASB).

Like newborn babies, long for the pure milk of the word, so that by it you may grow in respect to salvation (1 Peter 2:2, NASB).

How great are Your works, O Lord! Your thoughts are very deep (Ps. 92:5, NASB).

Praise

If the truth were to be known, praise itself would be enough to pray without ceasing.

> "Who is like unto Thee, O Lord, among the gods? Who is like Thee, glorious in holiness, fearful in praises, doing wonders?" (Exod. 15:11, KJ21).

> You, Lord, are all I have, and you give me all I need; my future is in your hands. How wonderful are your gifts to me; how good they are! (Ps. 16:5, 6, GNT).

> Your word is a lamp to guide me and a light for my path.... Accept my prayer of thanks, O Lord, and teach me your commands (Ps. 119:105, 108, GNT).

The Final Sleep

We live in a day and age when it is more important than ever to know the truth about those we long to see again.

> For the living know that they shall die: but the dead know not anything, neither have they any more a

> reward; for the memory of them is forgotten. Also their love, and their hatred, and their envy, is now perished; neither have they any more a portion for ever in any thing that is done under the sun (Eccl. 9:5, 6).

> Man dies and lies prostrate. Man expires, and where is he? As water evaporates from the sea, and a river becomes parched and dried up, so man lies down and does not rise. Until the heavens are no longer, he will not awake nor be aroused out of his sleep (Job 14:10-12, NASB).

> You are dust, and to dust you shall return (Gen. 3:19, NASB).

> Many of them that sleep in the dust of the earth shall awake (Dan. 12:2).

> For the trumpet shall sound, and the dead shall be raised incorruptible, and we shall be changed (1 Cor. 15:52).

The Spirituality of the Law

His commandments are a tool to open our eyes to our great need of Him.

> You shall be holy, for I the Lord your God am holy (Lev. 19:2, NASB).
>
> The Son of God appeared for this purpose, to destroy the works of the devil (1 John 3:8, NASB).
>
> His commandments are not burdensome. For whatever is born of God overcomes the world (1 John 5:3, 4, NASB).
>
> He has given us this command: Whoever loves God must also love his brother (1 John 4:21, NIV).

Listening to Prophecy

We live in a great time in prophetic history—the much anticipated rescue from sin. It is imperative that we learn about prophecy and understand its message for us.

> It is He who reveals the profound and hidden things ... There is a God in heaven who reveals mysteries (Dan. 2:22, 28, NASB).
>
> Let no man deceive you by any means: for that day shall not come, except there come a falling away

> first, and that man of sin be revealed, the son of perdition; ... Even him, whose coming is after the working of Satan with all power and signs and lying wonders, and with all deceivableness of unrighteousness in them that perish; because they received not the love of the truth, that they might be saved (2 Thess. 2:3, 9, 10).

> Blessed is he who reads and those who hear the words of the prophecy, and heed the things which are written in it; for the time is near (Rev. 1:3, NASB).

Dangerous Delusions—The World's Mark of Authority

Devotion to Jesus is the only remedy to delusion.

> I am afraid that, as the serpent deceived Eve by his craftiness, your minds will be led away from the simplicity and purity of devotion to Christ (2 Cor. 11:3, NASB).

> Yes, truth is lacking; and he who turns aside from evil makes himself a prey (Isa. 59:15, NASB).

> For the mystery of lawlessness is already at work (2 Thess. 2:7, NASB).

> But the court will sit for judgment, and his dominion will be taken away, annihilated and destroyed forever (Dan. 7:26, NASB).

> Hold fast what you have, so that no one will take your crown (Rev. 3:11, NASB).

The Church—God's Family

The whole plan of salvation is all about reuniting God's family.

> Where it is said to them, "You are not My people," it will be said to them, "You are the sons of the living God" (Hosea 1:10, NASB).

> I will also have compassion on her who had not obtained compassion, and I will say to those who were not My people, 'You are my people!' and they will say, 'You are my God!' (Hosea 2:23, NASB).

About His Business

Jesus was ever mindful of His heavenly Father's biddings.

> Wist ye not that I must be about my Father's business? (Luke 2:49).

> Jesus ... was moved with compassion toward them, because they were as sheep not having a shepherd: and he began to teach them many things (Mark 6:34).

> And all the people would get up early in the morning to come to Him in the temple to listen to Him (Luke 21:38, NASB).

The Blood of the Eternal Covenant

We must look to Christ's sacrifice and His blood if we want forgiveness for our sins.

> All things are cleansed with blood, and without shedding of blood there is no forgiveness (Heb. 9:22, NASB).

> For the life of the flesh is in the blood ... it is the blood by reason

of the life that makes atonement (Lev. 17:11, NASB).

He shall ... sprinkle [His blood] on the mercy seat and in front of the mercy seat (Lev. 16:15, NASB).

"This cup which is poured out for you is the new covenant in My blood" (Luke 22:20, NASB).

But with precious blood, as of a lamb unblemished and spotless, the blood of Christ (1 Peter 1:19, NASB).

... the God of peace, ... brought up from the dead the great Shepherd of the sheep through the blood of the eternal covenant, even Jesus our Lord (Heb. 13:20, NASB).

9

Assurance for This Time

The twenty-first century upheavals of this earth are not just geographical, they are also economical, emotional, and moral, to name a few. But the Lord promises to be with us, even to the end of the world. How may we insure that this promise is fulfilled in our lives? What else did He say that we need to know?

Jesus said, "Eat My flesh and drink My blood." Since He is the Word made flesh, we may do this by ingesting the words of the Bible. Perhaps there is more to this practice of memorizing scripture than first meets the eye. Even though we do not understand completely, we may move forward in faith, faith in Jesus and His words: "It is written, 'Man shall not live on bread alone, but on every word that proceeds out of the mouth of God" (Matt. 4:4, NASB).

Don't be Afraid

I realize that my unresponsiveness to the Lord is always based on fear. So in order to fulfill His hopes for me, I sought a balm for this blistering condition.

> And He said to them, "Why are you afraid? Do you still have no faith?" (Mark 4:40, NASB).

> For I the Lord thy God will hold thy

> right hand, saying unto thee, Fear not; I will help thee (Isa. 41:13).

> When you pass through the waters, I will be with you; ... When you walk through the fire, you will not be scorched (Isa. 43:2, NASB).

> But if your enemy is hungry, feed him, and if he is thirsty, give him a drink ... Do not be overcome by evil, but overcome evil with good (Rom. 12:20, 21, NASB).

> For God so loved the world, that he gave his only begotten Son, that whosoever believeth in him should not perish, but have everlasting life (John 3:16).

> My flesh and my heart may fail, but God is the strength of my heart and my portion forever (Ps. 73:26, NASB).

The Feast

The Lord is even now preparing the joys of eternity.

> The kingdom of heaven may be compared to a king who gave a wedding

> feast for his son (Matt. 22:2, NASB).

> While they were eating, Jesus took some bread, and after a blessing, He broke it and gave it to the disciples, and said, "Take eat; this is My body." And when He had taken a cup and given thanks, He gave it to them, saying, "Drink from it, all of you; for this is My blood of the covenant, which is poured out for many for forgiveness of sins. But I say to you, I will not drink of this fruit of this vine from now until that day when I drink it new with you in My Father's kingdom" (Matt. 26:26-29, NASB).

Deep Need

This is one of the first scripture messages I prayed for.

> Mine eyes fail for thy word, saying, When wilt thou comfort me? For I am become like a bottle in the smoke; yet do I not forget thy statutes (Ps. 119:82, 83).

> And the fields produce no food ... Yet I will exult in the Lord, I will rejoice in the God of my salvation

(Hab. 3:17, 18, NASB).

I believed, therefore have I spoken: I was greatly afflicted: I said in my haste, All men are liars (Ps. 116:10, 11).

Knowing that the testing of your faith produces endurance.... If any of you lacks wisdom, let him ask of God, who gives to all generously and without reproach, and it will be given to him (James 1:3, 5, NASB).

Counselor

In assembling these messages from scripture, I soon realized how willing our great Counselor is to give us the wisdom we need for each occasion.

Jesus called them to Himself and said, "You know that the rulers of the Gentiles lord it over them, and their great men exercise authority over them. It is not this way among you, but whoever wishes to become great among you shall be your servant (Matt. 20:25, 26, NASB).

I advise you to buy from Me gold refined by fire so that you may

> become rich, and white garments so that you may clothe yourself, and that the shame of your nakedness will not be revealed; and eye salve to anoint your eyes so that you may see (Rev. 3:18, NASB).

He Will Save Our Children

Praise the Lord for this promise!

> Thus says the Lord, "Restrain your voice from weeping and your eyes from tears; for your work will be rewarded," declares the Lord, "And they will return from the land of the enemy. There is hope for your future," declares the Lord, "And your children will return to their own territory" (Jer. 31:16, 17, NASB).

> "Do not fear, for I am with you; I will bring your offspring from the east, and gather you from the west. I will say to the north, 'Give them up!' And to the south, 'Do not hold them back!' Bring My sons from afar and My daughters from the ends of the earth, Everyone who is called by My name, and whom I have created for My glory, whom I have formed, even whom I have

made" (Isa. 43:5-7, NASB).

Wait on the Lord

Waiting is so important in our relationship with Jesus. It gives us time to set aside our pride and self-sufficiency and rely wholly on the Lord.

> Cast your burden upon the Lord and He will sustain you; He will never allow the righteous to be shaken (Ps. 55:22, NASB).
>
> The young lions do lack and suffer hunger; but they who seek the Lord shall not be in want of any good thing. Come, you children, listen to me (Ps. 34:10, 11, NASB).
>
> For the Lord God is a sun and shield: the Lord will give grace and glory: no good thing will he withhold from them that walk uprightly (Ps. 84:11).

Success

Yes, there is a proven recipe for success.

> If you abide in Me, and My words

> abide in you, ask whatever you wish, and it will be done for you (John 15:7, NASB).

> "Do not store up for yourselves treasures on earth, where moth and rust destroy ... But store up for yourselves treasures in heaven ... for where your treasure is, there your heart will be also (Matt. 6:19-21, NASB).

> Everyone who hears these words of Mine and acts on them, may be compared to a wise man who built his house on the rock (Matt. 7:24, NASB).

The Cup of Youth

Youth have their whole life ahead of them, but may they understand the importance of each decision in forming their future.

> Behold, I was shapen in iniquity; and in sin did my mother conceive me (Ps. 51:5).

> The Lord is good to those who wait for Him, to the person who seeks Him. It is good that he waits silently for the salvation of the Lord. It

> is good for a man that he should bear the yoke in his youth. Let him sit alone and be silent since He has laid it on him (Lam. 3:25-28, NASB).
>
> How blessed is the man who does not walk in the counsel of the wicked (Ps. 1:1, NASB).

Free at Last

The day is coming soon when we will be free at last—free from the usurpation of sin.

> "These who are clothed in the white robes, who are they, and where have they come from?" … "These are the ones who come out of the great tribulation, and they have washed their robes and made them white in the blood of the Lamb.... for the Lamb in the center of the throne will be their shepherd, and will guide them to springs of the water of life; and God will wipe every tear from their eyes (Rev. 7:13-17, NASB).
>
> And there shall be no more death, neither sorrow, nor crying, neither shall there be any more pain: for

> the former things are passed away (Rev. 21:4).

From Sorrow to Song

We have a price to pay for our happiness: being willing to part with the cost of sin.

> They that sow in tears shall reap in joy (Ps. 126:5, KJ21).

> Turn from these vain things to a living God (Acts 14:15, NASB).

> We are the temple of the living God ... "Therefore ... do not touch what is unclean; and I will welcome you. And I will be a father to you, and you shall be sons and daughters to Me," says the Lord Almighty. Therefore, having these promises, beloved, let us cleanse ourselves from all defilement of flesh and spirit, perfecting holiness in the fear of God (2 Cor. 6:16-18, 7:1, NASB).

> Giving all diligence, add to your faith virtue; and to virtue knowledge; and to knowledge temperance; and to temperance patience; and to patience godliness; and

> to godliness brotherly kindness; and to brotherly kindness charity (2 Peter 1:5-7).

His Fountain, Our Foundation

Jesus' birth was just the beginning of the steady tide of love to wash over this world.

> She wrapped Him in cloths, and laid Him in a manger, because there was no room for them in the inn (Luke 2:7, NASB).

> But Pilate said to them, "Why, what evil has He done?" But they shouted all the more, "Crucify Him!" (Mark 15:14, NASB).

> He poured out Himself to death, and was numbered with the transgressors (Isa. 53:12, NASB).

> When they came to the place called The Skull, there they crucified Him and the criminals ... But Jesus was saying, "Father, forgive them; for they do not know what they are doing" (Luke 23:33, 34, NASB).

> At the ninth hour Jesus cried out

> with a loud voice ... "My God, My God, why have You forsaken Me?" (Mark 15:34, NASB).

> Our old self was crucified with Him, in order that our body of sin might be done away with, so that we would no longer be slaves to sin (Rom. 6:6, NASB).

Spiritual Gifts

Do we appreciate what the spiritual gifts are capable of?

> For you know that it was not with perishable things such as silver or gold that you were redeemed from the empty way of life handed down to you from your forefathers, but with the precious blood of Christ (1 Peter 1:18, 19, NIV).

> Above all, keep fervent in your love for one another ... As each one has received a special gift, employ it in serving one another (1 Peter 4:8, 10, NASB).

10

Teach Me to Pray

A rose by any other name would smell as sweet. Prayer ascends with the intense saturation of the richest and best-blended incense to the throne of God. Where is His throne? It is where Jesus is ministering from to heal our sin-ridden lives. Prayer opens the throne room of the heart to God. We need not be embarrassed to let God know what we wish we could erase forever. He already knows. He is waiting to erase it, to throw it into the bottom of the sea.

Rags to Riches

As we turn from the claims of the world, the scales will fall from our eyes, and we will seek after Christ and the eternal riches He offers.

> All our righteous deeds are like a filthy garment; and all of us wither like a leaf, and our iniquities, like the wind, take us away (Isa. 64:6, NASB).

> Cast me not away from thy presence; and take not thy holy spirit from me (Ps. 51:11).

> "I have spread out My hands all day long to a rebellious people, who walk in the way which is not good, following their own thoughts

(Isa. 65:2, NASB).

There is a way which seems right to a man, but its end is the way of death (Prov. 14:12, NASB).

Trust in the Lord with all your heart, and lean not on your own understanding; in all your ways acknowledge him, and he will make your paths straight. Do not be wise in your own eyes; fear the Lord and shun evil. This will bring health to your body and nourishment to your bones (Prov. 3:5-8, NIV).

Words to Speak

Instead of being quick to speak and slow to listen, the Lord asks us to be quick to listen and slow to speak.

> Restore to me the joy of Your salvation and sustain me with a willing spirit. Then I will teach transgressors Your ways, and sinners will be converted to You (Ps. 51:12, 13, NASB).

> How sweet are Your words to my taste! Yes, sweeter than honey to my mouth! (Ps. 119:103, NASB).

> What a joy it is to find just the right word for the right occasion! (Prov. 15:23, GNT).

For Children and Others

Glorious present-day saints, stay true to your beliefs and desire the ornaments of a meek and quiet spirit.

> Open their eyes so that they may turn from darkness to light and from the dominion of Satan to God, that they may receive forgiveness of sins and an inheritance among

> those who have been sanctified by faith in Me (Acts 26:18, NASB).

> That Christ may dwell in your hearts by faith; that ye ... might be filled with all the fulness of God (Eph. 3:17-19).

> So that you will walk in a manner worthy of the Lord, to please Him in all respects ... For He rescued us from the domain of darkness, and transferred us to the kingdom of His beloved Son, in whom we have redemption, the forgiveness of sins (Col. 1:10-14, NASB).

Fiery Darts

The intensity of emotional pain makes us very vulnerable to bitterness, but there is no need to take action. The Lord is the only One who has the skill to intervene.

> When my heart was embittered and I was pierced within, then I was senseless and ignorant; I was like a beast before You. Nevertheless I am continually with You; You have taken hold of my right hand. With Your counsel You will guide me (Ps. 73:21-24, NASB).

> In the shadow of Your wings I take refuge until destruction passes by (Ps. 57:1, NASB).

From Trial to Victory

We are told that the angels delight to be part of the work to uplift and deliver us.

> O My Father, if it be possible, let this cup pass from me: nevertheless not as I will, but as thou wilt (Matt. 26:39).

> He was ... with the wild beasts; and the angels ministered unto him (Mark 1:13).

> Blessed be the God ... who has sent His angel and delivered His servants who put their trust in Him, violating the king's command and yielded up their bodies so as not to serve or worship any god except their own God (Dan. 3:28, NASB).

> "Your God whom you constantly serve will Himself deliver you" (Dan. 6:16, NASB).

Come Boldly and Seek His Will

Under even the most forlorn circumstances, the Lord bids us sit at His feet.

> 'I know the plans that I have for you,' declares the Lord, 'plans for welfare and not calamity to give you a future and a hope. Then you will call upon Me and come and pray to Me, and I will listen to you. You will ... find Me when you search for Me with all your heart (Jer. 29:11-13, NASB).

> Let us therefore come boldly unto the throne of grace, that we may obtain mercy, and find grace to help in time of need (Heb. 4:16).

Management

Have you ever wondered what the secret is to being able to manage your resources wisely? The answer is found in three words—tithes and offerings.

> The earth is the Lord's, and all it contains (Ps. 24:1, NASB).

> He chose to give us birth through the word of truth, that we might be

a kind of firstfruits of all he created (James 1:18, NIV).

You shall remember the Lord your God, for it is He who is giving you power to make wealth, that He may confirm His covenant (Deut. 8:18, NASB).

Yield to Hope

Even though departing from evil and staying loyal to God makes us a target and we may think all will be lost, these are the times we need to hold on to the promises of His care.

Why are you in despair, O my soul? And why have you become disturbed within me? Hope in God, for I shall again praise Him for the help of His presence (Ps. 42:5, NASB).

Have no fear of sudden disaster or of the ruin that overtakes the wicked (Prov. 3:25, NIV).

For God hath not given us the spirit of fear, but of power and of love and of a sound mind (2 Tim. 1:7, KJ21).

Because the Sovereign Lord helps me, I will not be disgraced.

> Therefore have I set my face like flint, and I know I will not be put to shame (Isa. 50:7, NIV).

The Human Condition

I don't know about you, but I always expect others to be better than me, and when they are not, I am disappointed. Is that fair? I should concentrate on what the Lord can do not on what others should do.

> But you, dear friends, build yourselves up in your most holy faith and pray in the Holy Spirit. Keep yourselves in God's love as you wait for the mercy of our Lord Jesus Christ to bring you to eternal life. Be merciful to those who doubt; snatch others from the fire and save them; to others show mercy, mixed with fear—hating even the clothing stained by corrupted flesh (Jude 20-23, NIV).

> You hypocrite, first take the log out of your own eye, and then you will see clearly to take out the speck that is in your brother's eye (Luke 6:42, NASB).

A Heavenly Place—The Sanctuary

The deepest longing of the human soul is for reconciliation with our Creator.

> [Jesus] has taken His seat at the right hand of the throne of the Majesty in the heavens (Heb. 8:1, NASB).

> At night my soul longs for You, indeed, my spirit within me seeks You diligently; for when the earth experiences Your judgments, the inhabitants of the world learn righteousness (Isa. 26:9, NASB).

> To love him with all the heart, and with all the understanding, and with all the soul, and with all the strength, and to love his neighbour as himself, is more than all whole burnt offerings and sacrifices (Mark 12:33).

> May He send you help from the sanctuary (Ps. 20:2, NASB).

Evening, Morning, and Noon

We may stay attuned to the Spirit of God by

having regular times to refresh our faith.

> [Daniel] continued kneeling on his knees three times a day, praying and giving thanks before his God (Dan. 6:10, NASB).

> Daniel replied with discretion and discernment (Dan. 2:14, NASB).

> Evening, and morning, and at noon, will I pray (Ps. 55:17).

Ask for Answers

The Lord watches out for us. But He also hopes that we will ask Him for answers because this shows Him that we trust Him.

> If any of you lacks wisdom, let him ask of God, who gives to all generously and without reproach, and it will be given to him (James 1:5, NASB).

> Do not be worried about your life, as to what you will eat or what you will drink; nor for your body, as to what you will put on. Is not life more than food, and the body more than clothing?... But seek first His kingdom and His righteousness,

> and all these things will be added to you. So do not worry about tomorrow (Matt. 6:25-34, NASB).

> Wisdom is the principal thing; therefore get wisdom: and with all thy getting get understanding (Prov. 4:7).

Guidance

Jesus wants to guide us into restoration of His image in His dear human family.

> "Everything is permissible"—but not everything is beneficial.... Nobody should seek his own good, but the good of others (1 Cor. 10:23, 24, NIV).

> Ye are the light of the world. A city that is set on an hill cannot be hid.... Let your light so shine before men, that they may see your good works, and glorify your Father which is in heaven (Matt. 5:14, 16).

> We must work the works of Him who sent Me as long as it is day; night is coming when no one can work (John 9:4, NASB).

Deliverance

The secret to deliverance is keeping our eyes on Jesus.

> Unto Thee, O Lord, do I lift up my soul; O my God, I trust in thee: let me not be ashamed, let not mine enemies triumph over me....
>
> Shew me thy ways, O Lord; teach me thy paths.... The secret of the Lord is with them that fear him; and he will shew them his covenant.
>
> Mine eyes are ever toward the Lord; for he shall pluck my feet out of the net.... O keep my soul, and deliver me: let me not be ashamed; for I put my trust in thee (Ps 25:1-20, KJV).

Restored

When the walls are closing in around me and I don't know what happened, this is my prayer.

> Our Father which art in heaven, Hallowed be thy name (Matt. 6:9, KJV).

> I know my transgressions, and my sin is ever before me. Against You, You only, I have sinned and done what is evil in your sight, so that You are justified when You speak and blameless when You judge....
>
> Hide Your face from my sins and blot out all my iniquities. Create in me a clean heart, O God, and renew a steadfast spirit within me.
>
> Do not cast me away from Your presence and do not take your Holy Spirit from me. Restore to me the joy of Your salvation and sustain me with a willing spirit (Ps. 51:3-12, NASB).
>
> Deliver us from evil: For thine is the kingdom, and the power, and the glory, for ever. Amen (Matt. 6:13, KJV).

Not My Strength But Yours

When you know your physical strength is minus ten and counting, or any other time for that matter, He will share His strength with you.

> He looked down from His holy

height; from heaven the Lord gazed upon the earth, to hear the groaning of the prisoner, to set free those who were doomed to death (Ps. 102:19, 20. NASB).

The law of the Spirit of life in Christ Jesus hath made me free from the law of sin and death.... That the righteousness of the law might be fulfilled in us, who walk not after the flesh, but after the Spirit (Rom. 8:2, 4).

He giveth power to the faint; and to them that have no might he increaseth strength. Even the youths shall faint and be weary, and the young men shall utterly fall: But they that wait upon the Lord shall renew their strength; they shall mount up with wings as eagles; they shall run, and not be weary; and they shall walk, and not faint (Isa. 40:29-31).

11

Healing Our Hearts

When God fills our heart, everything from the deepest thirst in our souls to the way we spend our time will receive a splendid makeover. It may seem that everything is topsy-turvy at first, but after continued discipleship, things will start to fall into place. Not only will we benefit from this renewed relationship with God, but those around us will experience the difference. As we become more like Christ our desire to reach the lost will naturally increase. Let us trust Him to touch the hearts of those around us and be ready and willing to do His bidding to nurture, protect, and water the seedlings of faith and interest in their lives.

The Great Physician

Jesus is my doctor, and I must say there is none so skilled, knowledgeable, gentle, and kind as He.

> Jesus stopped and called them, and said, "What do you want Me to do for you?" (Matt. 20:32, NASB).

> Heal me, O Lord, and I shall be healed; save me, and I shall be saved: for thou art my praise (Jer. 17:14).

> Though I walk in the midst of trouble, You will revive me (Ps. 138:7, NASB).

> "For you will go out with joy and be led forth with peace ... Instead of the thorn bush the cypress will come up, and instead of the nettle the myrtle will come up" (Isa. 55:12, 13, NASB).

> 'I will restore you to health and I will heal you of your wounds,' declares the Lord (Jer. 30:17, NASB).

His Side

It is our afflictions that burn away the impurities and make us pliable for Him to apply His Word to our lives.

> He showed them both His hands and His side (John 20:20, NASB).

> The Father of mercies and God of all comfort, who comforts us in all our afflictions so that we will be able to comfort those who are in any affliction with the comfort with which we ourselves are comforted by God (2 Cor. 1:3, 4, NASB).

> [He] made us adequate as servants of a new covenant, not of the letter but of the Spirit; for the letter kills, but the Spirit gives life (2 Cor. 3:5, 6, NASB).

Mercy

When you find out about an illness and your life turns upside down, it is hard to know which way is up. But God's mercy and love are always present.

> Save me, O God, for the waters have threatened my life. I have sunk in deep mire, and there is no foothold ... Reproach has broken my heart and I am so sick. And I looked for sympathy, but there was none ... I am afflicted and in pain; may Your salvation, O God, set me securely on high.... You who seek God, let your heart revive. For the Lord hears the needy and does not despise His who are prisoners (Ps 69:1-33, NASB).

Carry His Cross for Others to See

To be free from petty frustrations means we

have strength and focus to be His witness.

> If when you do right and suffer for it you patiently endure it, this finds favor with God. For you have been called for this purpose, since Christ also suffered for you ... follow in His steps, who committed no sin, nor was any deceit found in His mouth; and while being reviled, He did not revile in return; while suffering, He uttered no threats, but kept entrusting Himself to Him who judges righteously (1 Peter 2:20-23, NASB).

> And the peace of God, which surpasses all comprehension, will guard your hearts and your minds in Christ Jesus (Phil. 4:7, NASB).

> So we too might walk in newness of life (Rom. 6:4, NASB).

Forgiveness

Forgiveness is what keeps the human soul from reeling into the oblivion of bitterness and seemingly irreconcilable differences.

> He is able to save completely those who come to God through him

(Heb. 7:25, NIV).

Come near to God and he will come near to you (James 4:8, NIV).

The wisdom that comes from heaven is first of all pure; then peace-loving, considerate, submissive, full of mercy and good fruit, impartial and sincere (James 3:17, NIV).

So, as those who have been chosen of God, holy and beloved, put on a heart of compassion, kindness, humility, gentleness and patience, bearing with one another, and forgiving each other, whoever has a complaint against anyone; just as the Lord forgave you, so also should you (Col. 3:12, 13, NASB).

Bear ye one another's burdens, and so fulfil the law of Christ (Gal. 6:2).

Your Hand Upon Me

We have inherited and cultivated harmful habits. We need God to reveal these to us.

O Lord, thou hast searched me, and known me.... Thou compassest my path and my lying down,

> and art acquainted with all my ways.... Thou hast beset me behind and before, and laid thine hand upon me....
>
> Search me, O God, and know my heart: try me, and know my thoughts: and see if there be any wicked way in me, and lead me in the way everlasting (Ps. 139).

Doubt Is Death; Belief Is Life

I am so glad the story of the unbelieving father is included in the gospels.

> The one who doubts is like the surf of the sea, driven and tossed by the wind. For that man ought not to expect that he will receive anything from the Lord (James 1:6, 7, NASB).
>
> [And the father said,] "But if You can do anything, take pity on us and help us!" And Jesus said to him, "'If You can?' All things are possible to him who believes." Immediately the boy's father cried out and said, "I do believe; help my

> unbelief" (Mark 9:22-24, NASB).

> When you received the word of God which you heard from us, you accepted it not as the word of men, but for what it really is, the word of God, which also performs its work in you who believe (1 Thess. 2:13, NASB).

> While ye have Light, believe in the Light, that ye may be the children of Light (John 12:36, KJ21).

The Promise of Bread

Bread has so much potential. Just think how much nutrition can be packed into a homemade loaf ... just about anything you want your family to eat.

> You shall serve the Lord your God, and He will bless your bread and your water; and I will remove sickness from your midst (Exod. 23:25, NASB).

> "My people will be satisfied with My goodness," declares the Lord (Jer. 31:14, NASB).

> "The bread of God is he who comes

> down from heaven and gives life to the world."... Jesus declared, "I am the bread of life. He who comes to me will never go hungry" (John 6:33, 35 NIV).

The Lord Is My Portion

Pride is so inappropriate. We need the Lord's strength to help us think and act without sin.

> The Lord is my portion (Ps. 119:57, NASB).

> Not to us, O Lord, not to us, but to Your name give glory because of Your lovingkindness, because of Your truth (Ps. 115:1, NASB).

> The Lord's lovingkindnesses indeed never cease, for His compassions never fail. They are new every morning; Great is Your faithfulness (Lam. 3:22, 23, NASB).

Health

My grandfather told me once that nothing is impossible for God. Even with issues of health, He can restore us to a life made whole.

> A righteous man may have many troubles, but the Lord delivers him from them all (Ps. 34:19, NIV).
>
> In my distress I called to the Lord, and he answered me. From the depths of the grave I called for help, and you listened to my cry (Jonah 2:2, NIV).
>
> Though the Lord be high, yet hath He respect unto the lowly ... Though I walk in the midst of trouble, Thou wilt revive me (Ps. 138:6, 7, KJ21).
>
> Praise the Lord, O my soul ... and forget not all his benefits—who forgives all your sins and heals all your diseases, who redeems your life from the pit and crowns you with love and compassion, who satisfies your desires with good things, so that your youth is renewed like the eagle's (Ps. 103:1-5, NIV).
>
> For I have satiated the weary soul, and I have replenished every

> sorrowful soul (Jer. 31:25, KJ21).

A Heart for Others

Jesus is the only example of real love that this world has.

> I go to prepare a place for you (John 14:2, NASB).

> I will not leave you as orphans (John 14:18, NASB).

> Let not your heart be troubled, nor let it be afraid (John 14:27, NASB).

> My kindness shall not depart from thee, neither shall the covenant of my peace be removed, saith the Lord that hath mercy on thee (Isa. 54:10).

> These things have I spoken unto you, that my joy might remain in you, and that your joy might be full.... love one another, as I have loved you (John 15:11, 12).

King of the Eternal

Remember, He is not only the King of this

world but of eternity.

> He who reaps is receiving wages and is gathering fruit for life eternal; so that he who sows and he who reaps may rejoice together (John 4:36, NASB).

> Let him who does right continue to do right; and let him who is holy continue to be holy (Rev. 22:11, NIV).

> Blessed are they that do his commandments, that they may have right to the tree of life, and may enter in through the gates into the city (Rev. 22:14).

Prepare to be Simple

Apparently more is not better.

> "Please test your servants for ten days, and let us be given some vegetables to eat and water to drink.... So the overseer continued to withhold their choice food and the wine they were to drink, and kept giving them vegetables. As for these four youths, God gave them knowledge and intelligence in every branch of

> literature and wisdom; Daniel even understood all kinds of visions and dreams (Dan. 1:12-17, NASB).

> The ravens brought [Elijah] bread and meat in the morning and bread and meat in the evening, and he would drink from the brook (1 Kings 17:6, NASB).

> Blessed are you ... whose princes eat at the appropriate time—for strength and not for drunkenness (Eccl. 10:17, NASB).

His Voice

Life consists of the here and now, and we need to make the most of each day.

> The Lord longs to be gracious to you, and therefore He waits on high to have compassion on you. For the Lord is a God of justice; how blessed are all those who long for Him.... Your ears will hear a word behind you, [saying,] "This is the way, walk in it" (Isa. 30:18, 21, NASB).

> "Today if you hear His voice, Do not harden your hearts" (Heb. 3:7, 8, NASB).

Hope

What a blessed day that will be when Jesus returns to take us home!

> When the Lord brought back the captive ones of Zion, we were like those who dream. Then our mouth was filled with laughter and our tongue with joyful shouting ... The Lord has done great things for us. We are glad (Ps. 126:1-3, NASB).

> May he vindicate the afflicted of the people, save the children of the needy and crush the oppressor (Ps. 72:4, NASB).

> Now the God of hope fill you with all joy and peace in believing, that ye may abound in hope, through the power of the Holy Ghost (Rom. 15:13).

The Miracle of Nature

The very availability of natural remedies speaks of how God has provided for our needs.

> Purge me with hyssop, and I shall be clean (Ps. 51:7).

> No longer drink water exclusively, but use a little wine [grape juice] for the sake of your stomach and your frequent ailments (1 Tim. 5:23, NASB).

> A man that is called Jesus made clay, and anointed mine eyes, and said unto me, Go to the pool of Siloam, and wash: and I went and washed, and I received sight (John 9:11).

> "My father, had the prophet told you to do some great thing, would you not have done it? How much more then, when he says to you, 'Wash, and be clean'?" (2 Kings 5:13, NASB).

Born to Belong

We are born to belong to the King of kings and Lord of lords.

> If we confess our sins, he is faithful and just to forgive us our sins, and to cleanse us from all unrighteousness (1 John 1:9).

> To Him who loves us and released us from our sins by His blood (Rev. 1:5, 6, NASB).

> Of Him all the prophets bear witness that through His name everyone who believes in Him receives forgiveness of sins (Acts 10:43, NASB).

> Jesus stood and cried out, saying, "If anyone is thirsty, let him come to Me and drink" (John 7:37, NASB).

> He who eats My flesh and drinks My blood abides in Me, and I in him.... It is the Spirit who gives life; the flesh profits nothing; the words that I have spoken to you are spirit and are life (John 6:56, 63, NASB).

> His eyes are a flame of fire, and on His head are many diadems ... And on His robe and on His thigh He has a name written, "King of Kings, and Lord of Lords" (Rev. 19:12, 16, NASB).

Grief

With grief, hope is the only relief. Come, Lord Jesus.

> "My God, My God, why have You forsaken Me?" (Matt. 27:46, NASB).

He placed His right hand on me, saying, "Do not be afraid; I am the first and the last, and the living One; and I was dead, and behold, I am alive forevermore, and I have the keys of death and of Hades" (Rev. 1:17, 18, NASB).

He will wipe away every tear from their eyes; and there will no longer be any death; there will no longer be any mourning, or crying, or pain; the first things have passed away (Rev. 21:4, NASB).

12

The True Witness

A state of hope and eager anticipation of the Lord's return and the eternal blessings He has in store for us is the treasure of the true witness. As His followers, we know He surely will use us to reach other people. So like the fire department, we remain at attention, ready to answer the call of "fire." We are first responders, going forward with the angels who encamp around us and our leader the Holy Spirit to softly and tenderly part the darkness and to bind the wounds of others. We are God's witness that He is who He says He is.

The Great Controversy

We don't like to speak of it, but, yes, there are people we are not to trust.

> Certain men whose condemnation was written about long ago have secretly slipped in among you. They are godless men, who change the grace of our God into a license for immorality and deny Jesus Christ our only Sovereign and Lord (Jude 4, NIV).

> This people draw near with their words and honor Me with their lip service, but they remove their hearts far from Me, and their reverence for Me consists of tradition

learned by rote (Isa. 29:13, NASB).

But you beloved ... keep yourselves in the love of God (Jude 20, 21, NASB).

Greater love has no one than this, that one lay down his life for his friends (John 15:13, NASB).

But God demonstrates His own love toward us, in that while we were yet sinners, Christ died for us (Rom. 5:8, NASB).

I will even look eagerly for Him (Isa. 8:17, NASB).

Marriage and the Family

Marriage was designed in the Garden of Eden.

> Behold, I am the Lord, the God of all flesh: is there any thing too hard for me? (Jer. 32:27).

> I will make an everlasting covenant with them, that I will not turn away from them, to do them good; but I will put my fear in their hearts, that they shall not depart from me. (Jer. 32:40).

> 'For I will pour out water on the thirsty land and streams on the dry ground; I will pour out My Spirit on your offspring and My blessing on your descendants; and they will spring up among the grass like poplars by streams of water.' "This one will say, 'I am the Lord's'; and that one will call on the name of Jacob; and another will write on his hand, 'Belonging to the Lord,' and will name Israel's name with honor (Isa. 44:3-5, NASB).

> Offer to God a sacrifice of thanksgiving and pay your vows to the

> Most High; Call upon Me in the day of trouble; I shall rescue you, and you will honor me (Ps. 50:14, 15, NASB).

Creation

Since His Word can create, what can it do for us?

> Then God said, "Let Us make man in Our image, according to Our likeness.... God created man in His own image, in the image of God He created him; male and female He created them (Gen. 1:26, 27, NASB).

Loyalty

Some things are becoming archaic, but hopefully loyalty is not one of them.

> I delight in loyalty rather than sacrifice (Hosea 6:6, NASB).

> Love does no wrong to a neighbor; therefore love is the fulfillment of the law.... Let us behave properly as in the day, not in carousing and drunkenness, not in sexual

> promiscuity and sensuality, not in strife and jealousy. But put on the Lord Jesus Christ, and make no provision for the flesh in regard to its lusts (Rom. 13:10-14, NASB).

The Kingdom of Heaven

Yes! Purity and goodness will prevail, and in the end, God will establish His kingdom on this earth.

> All things are cleansed with blood, and without shedding of blood there is no forgiveness (Heb. 9:22, NASB).

> These are they which came out of great tribulation, and have washed their robes, and made them white in the blood of the Lamb (Rev. 7:14).

> Blessed are they that do his commandments, that they may have right to the tree of life, and may enter in through the gates into the city (Rev. 22:14).

> The twelve gates were twelve pearls, each gate made of a single pearl.... Nothing impure will ever enter into it, nor will anyone who does what is

> shameful or deceitful (Rev. 21:21, 27, NIV).

Sow Truths as the Gardener

Remember, the words we speak have power for life or for death.

> The Lord God has given Me the tongue of disciples, that I may know how to sustain the weary one with a word. He awakens Me morning by morning, He awakens My ear to listen as a disciple. The Lord God has opened My ear; and I was not disobedient nor did I turn back (Isa. 50:4, 5, NASB).

> Preach the word; be ready in season and out of season (2 Tim. 4:2, NASB).

His Will: I Surrender All

Love is extreme surrender for another's welfare. And I choose to surrender all to be the servant of love.

> The prudent person keeps silent, for it is an evil time. Seek good and not evil, that you may live; and thus

> may the Lord God of hosts be with you (Amos 5:13, 14, NASB).

> For indeed He was crucified because of weakness, yet He lives because of the power of God. For we also are weak in Him, yet we will live with Him because of the power of God directed toward you (2 Cor. 13:4, NASB).

> Love is patient, love is kind and is not jealous; love does not brag and is not arrogant ... [love] bears all things, believes all things, hopes all things, endures all things. Love never fails (1 Cor. 13:4-8, NASB).

Seek Those Living Without God

The lost are out there waiting for our invitation.

> The Sunrise from on high will visit us, to shine upon those who sit in darkness and the shadow of death (Luke 1:78, 79, NASB).

> The glory of the Lord shone around them ... But the angel said to them,

> ... "I bring you good news of great joy which will be for all the people" (Luke 2:9, 10, NASB).

> Let your light shine before men in such a way that they may see your good works, and glorify your Father who is in heaven (Matt. 5:16, NASB).

The Robe

The robe of Christ's righteousness is true luxury.

> You are clothed with splendor and majesty, covering Yourself with light as with a cloak (Ps. 104:1, 2, NASB).

> Let us lay aside the deeds of darkness and put on the armor of light (Rom. 12:13, NASB).

> I will rejoice greatly in the Lord, my soul will exult in my God; for He has clothed me with garments of salvation, He has wrapped me with a robe of righteousness (Isa. 61:10, NASB).

13

His Word, My Well-Being

The Lord is our Counselor. He knows how to guide us in all matters. Even amidst our burdens and pain, He honors our faith in Him with peace and joy. He knows how to provide for us right where we are and how to make us blossom as a rose in the desert. Lead on, O King of the eternal!

The Holy Spirit desires to teach us to know the things of God. It is with the Bible in our hands that we are best able to do this. Our hearts are softened by the beauty of the setting sun or from the healing touch of a friend. However, it is the Bible that teaches us understanding and reveals the answers to life's questions.

Knowing what Jesus says gives us faith. We need to continue feeding on His Word to keep the flame of faith burning. This keeps us peaceful at all times. It is by delighting in the goodness of the Lord that our desires are changed to match His. Thus, the life is turned around, and we have time to visit the sick and relieve the oppressed.

Our greatest reward is not in what He does for us, but how He does it. Whatever He does is best for us as well as the other people involved. He doesn't require that we locate more money—He promises to provide for our needs. But He does ask that we continue to turn our attention toward heaven. This means that when we pray, we need to be ready to be used to answer that prayer. There may seem as if there is no answer because God is waiting for us to do what He wants us to do.

Studying the Word helps us to surrender and humble ourselves to do His will—to let go and let God take control. Learning scripture is not about memorizing just to remember verses, but the goal is to soften our heart to the impressions of the Holy Spirit. Having our hearts prepared for the day allows us to think on the roses, not the thorns. Drinking from the fountain in the morning prepares us to be ready for His purposes for us during the day. Evening is a time for confession and thanksgiving for the events of the day. This also prepares us to receive the tender blessings He has for us in our waking moments the next morning.

This book was born out of a desire to make my own personalized set of Bible studies that would prepare people's hearts to attend an evangelistic series. I started collecting verses under different topics—need-based as well as doctrinal and the Holy Spirit mixed the two together. I pray the Lord will give us opportunities to share our knowledge of Him.

As I started applying scriptures to my life and following the Holy Spirit, I found clouds lifting and waves parting. The power of God manifested itself in my life. We are brainwashed into thinking that God is weak. It is not that God's power is weak in any way. But you have to experience it yourself long enough to make changes and to believe that His power is real.

I would encourage you to embark on this journey with someone you trust. That way you can help each other. And just remember, when the Lord fills your cup, there is always enough to share.

The Sanctuary

1. Psalm 29:9
2. Hosea 6:6
3. John 1:29
4. Exodus 25:8
5. Hebrews 8:1, 2

6. John 14:6
7. Hebrews 12:29
8. John 7:38, 39
9. Exodus 34:8-10
10. Revelation 21:1-7

The Word of God

1. Psalm 119:8-11, 89
2. Romans 11:33
3. Isaiah 59:15
4. Jeremiah 17:7, 8
5. John 1:1-5
6. Hebrews 5:13, 14
7. 1 Peter 1:22, 23
8. Luke 4:4
9. 1 Timothy 3:15, 16
10. Revelation 2:10

The Human Condition

1. Psalm 8:3-9
2. Acts 17:24-30
3. 1 Corinthians 15:21-26
4. Leviticus 19:18
5. Romans 1:18
6. John 15:10-27
7. James 2:1-10

8. 1 John 3:16-19
9. 2 Corinthians 7:1
10. Proverbs 4:18-27

Christ Our Leader

1. Genesis 1:26-28
2. Isaiah 9:1-7
3. Daniel 9:7-13
4. Luke 1:67-79
5. Matthew 5:1-24
6. Mark 2:13, 14
7. Luke 4:14-20
8. Revelation 1:17, 18
9. Revelation 21:3-7
10. Revelation 22:12

The Church and Its Mission

1. Ephesians 6:10-18
2. Hosea 2:23
3. 1 John 2:6
4. Ephesians 4:7-16
5. 1 Corinthians 10:31
6. 1 Peter 2:2-5
7. 1 Corinthians 12:12-31
8. Luke 9:59, 60
9. Revelation 7:13, 14

10. Revelation 14:4-12

The Family

1. Genesis 1:26-28
2. 1 Corinthians 11:3
3. Ephesians 5:21-33
4. Amos 3:3
5. 2 Corinthians 6:14, 15
6. 1 Corinthians 13:4-8
7. Colossians 3:18-21
8. 1 Peter 3:1, 7-10
9. 1 Corinthians 7:8-16
10. Jeremiah 31:3

The Spirituality of the Law

1. Romans 10:10
2. 1 John 3:4-6
3. Matthew 5:17, 18
4. Isaiah 42:21
5. James 2:8-17
6. Galatians 5:13-15
7. Psalm 119:142
8. Psalm 111:7, 8
9. Revelation 11:19
10. Micah 6:8

Dangerous Delusions

1. 2 Thessalonians 2:8-12
2. Revelation 13:13-15
3. James 3:14-18, 2:26
4. Genesis 3:1-5
5. Psalm 106:21-29
6. 1 Corinthians 10:20, 21
7. Revelation 16:13-19
8. Leviticus 19:31; 20:25, 26
9. Malachi 2:17; 3:1, 16-18
10. Revelation 3:10

Stewardship

1. Genesis 1:1
2. Psalm 24:1-5
3. Colossians 3:23-25
4. Ephesians 5:15-21
5. Luke 2:52
6. James 1:17
7. Deuteronomy 8:18
8. Leviticus 27:30
9. 1 Corinthians 9:7-14
10. 1 Chronicles 29:10-14

Clothed for Eternity

1. 1 Corinthians 13:1-13
2. Proverbs 28:13
3. John 12:32
4. 2 Corinthians 5:21
5. Ephesians 2:4-10
6. Titus 3:5
7. Philippians 3:7-11
8. Genesis 15:6
9. Zechariah 3:1-5
10. Revelation 3:18-21

Recommended Resources

Books:

- *Shadows of His Sacrifice* by Leslie Hardinge
- *Judge Me Please* by Gary Strunk
- *The Great Controversy* by Ellen G. White
- *Mind, Character and Personality* by Ellen G. White
- *Patriarchs and Prophets* by Ellen G. White
- *The Desire of Ages* by Ellen G. White

- *The Ministry of Healing* by Ellen G. White

Web sites:

- 3ABN.org
- SecretsUnsealed.org
- GospelMinistry.org
- GoAim.org
- 3AngelsTube.com
- Maranatha.org
- TEACHServices.com
- DesignersHealth.com

We invite you to view the complete
selection of titles we publish at:

www.AspectBooks.com

Scan with your mobile device to go directly to our website.

Please write or email us your praises, reactions, or thoughts about this or any other book we publish at:

ASPECT Books

www.ASPECTBooks.com

P.O. Box 954
Ringgold, GA 30736

info@AspectBooks.com

Aspect Books titles may be purchased in bulk for educational, business, fund-raising, or sales promotional use. For information, please e-mail:

BulkSales@AspectBooks.com

Finally, if you are interested in seeing your own book in print, please contact us at:

publishing@AspectBooks.com

We would be happy to review your manuscript for free.

CPSIA information can be obtained at www.ICGtesting.com
Printed in the USA
LVOW06s1829220713

343963LV00001B/15/P